Ultimate Keto Air Fryer Seafood Cookbook

Easy and Delicious Recipes

for a Balanced Lifestyle

Lucy Grant

reader will render any resulting actions solely under their purview. There are no scenarios in which the publisher or the original author of this work can be in any fashion deemed liable for any hardship or damages that may befall them after undertaking information described herein.

Additionally, the information in the following pages is intended only for informational purposes and should thus be thought of as universal. As befitting its nature, it is presented without assurance regarding its prolonged validity or interim quality. Trademarks that are mentioned are done without written consent and can in no way be considered an endorsement from the trademark holder.

Table of Contents

7

Introduction

What's the difference between an air fryer and deep fryer? Air fryers bake food at a high temperature with a high-powered fan, while deep fryers cook food in a vat of oil that has been heated up to a specific temperature. Both cook food quickly, but an air fryer requires practically zero preheat time while a deep fryer can take upwards of 10 minutes. Air fryers also require little to no oil and deep fryers require a lot that absorb into the food. Food comes out crispy and juicy in both appliances, but don't taste the same, usually because deep fried foods are coated in batter that cook differently in an air fryer vs a deep fryer. Battered foods needs to be sprayed with oil before cooking in an air fryer to help them color and get crispy, while the hot oil soaks into the batter in a deep fryer. Flour-based batters and wet batters don't cook well in an air fryer, but they come out very well in a deep fryer.

The ketogenic diet is one such example. The diet calls for a very small number of carbs to be eaten. This means food such as rice, pasta, and other starchy vegetables like potatoes are off the menu. Even relaxed versions of the keto diet minimize carbs to a large extent and this compromises the goals of many dieters. They end up having to exert large amounts of willpower to follow the diet. This doesn't do them any favors since willpower is like a muscle. At some point, it tires and this is when the dieter goes right back to their old pattern of eating. I have personal experience with this. In terms of health benefits, the keto diet offers the most. The reduction of carbs forces your body to mobilize fat and this results in automatic fat loss and better health.

Feel free to mix and match the recipes you see in here and play around with them. Eating is supposed to be fun! Unfortunately, we've associated fun eating with unhealthy food. This doesn't have to be the case. The air fryer, combined with the Mediterranean diet, will make your mealtimes fun-filled again and full of taste. There's no grease and messy cleanups to deal with anymore. Are you excited yet?

You should be! You're about to embark on a journey full of air fried goodness!

Easy Bacon Shrimp

Preparation Time: 10 minutes

Cooking Time: 7 minutes

Serve: 2

Ingredients:

8 shrimp, deveined

8 bacon slices Pepper

Directions:

Wrap shrimp with bacon slices.

Select Air Fry mode.

Set time to 7 minutes and temperature 390 F then press START.

The air fryer display will prompt you to ADD FOOD once the temperature is reached then place shrimp in the air fryer basket.

Season shrimp with pepper and serve.

Old Bay Crab Sticks with Garlic Mayo

Prep + Cook Time: 20 minutes 4

Servings

INGREDIENTS

1 lb crab sticks

1 tbsp old bay seasoning

⅓ cup panko breadcrumbs

2 eggs

½ cup mayonnaise

2 garlic cloves, minced

1 lime, juiced

1 cup flour

DIRECTIONS

Preheat air fryer to 390 F.

Beat the eggs in a bowl.

In another bowl, mix breadcrumbs with old bay seasoning.

In a third bowl, pour the flour.

Dip the sticks in the flour, then in the eggs, and finally in the crumbs.

Spray with cooking spray and AirFry in the frying basket for 12 minutes, flipping once.

Mix mayonnaise with garlic and lime juice.

Serve as a dip along with crab sticks.

Rosemary Cashew Shrimp

Prep + Cook Time: 35 minutes

4 Servings

INGREDIENTS

3 oz cashews, chopped

1 tbsp fresh rosemary, chopped

1 ½ lb shrimp

1 garlic clove, minced

1 tbsp breadcrumbs

1 egg, beaten

1 tbsp olive oil

Salt and black pepper to taste

DIRECTIONS

Preheat air fryer to 320 F.

Combine olive oil with garlic and brush onto the shrimp.

Combine rosemary, cashews, and crumbs in a bowl.

Dip shrimp in the egg and coat it in the cashew mixture.

Place in the frying basket and Bake for 25 minutes.

Increase the temperature to 390 F and cook for 5 more minutes.

Cover with a foil and let sit for a couple of minutes before serving.

Mediterranean Squid Rings with Couscous

Prep + Cook Time: 20 minutes

4 Servings

INGREDIENTS

1 cup couscous

1 lb squid rings

2 large eggs

½ cup all-purpose flour

½ cup semolina

1 tsp ground coriander seeds

1 tsp cayenne pepper

Salt and black pepper to taste

4 lemon wedges to garnish

DIRECTIONS

Place the couscous in a large bowl and cover with boiling water.

Season with salt and pepper and stir.

Cover and set aside for 5-7 minutes until the water is absorbed.

Preheat air fryer to 390 F.

Beat the eggs in a bowl.

In another bowl, combine the flour, semolina, ground coriander, cayenne pepper, salt, and pepper.

Dip the squid rings in the eggs first, then in the flour mixture, and place them in the greased frying basket.

AirFry for 15 minutes, until golden brown, shaking once.

Transfer the couscous to a large platter and arrange the squid rings on top.

Serve.

Cod Fillets with Ginger-Cilantro Sauce

Prep + Cook Time: 20 minutes

4 Servings

INGREDIENTS

1 lb cod fillets

2 tbsp fresh cilantro, chopped

Salt to taste

4 green onions, chopped

1 cup water

1 tbsp ginger paste

5 tbsp light soy sauce

2 tbsp olive oil

1 tsp soy sauce

2 cubes rock sugar

DIRECTIONS

Preheat air fryer to 360 F.

Sprinkle cod fillets with salt and some olive oil.

Place in the frying basket and AirFry for 15 minutes, flipping once halfway through.

Heat the remaining olive oil in a pan over medium heat and stir-fry the remaining ingredients for 4-5 minutes.

Pour the sauce over the fish and serve.

Gourmet Black Cod with Fennel & Pecans

Prep + Cook Time: 20 minutes

2 Servings

INGREDIENTS

2black cod fillets

Salt and black pepper to taste

1 small fennel bulb, sliced

½ cup pecans

2 tsp white balsamic vinegar

2 tbsp olive oil

DIRECTIONS

Preheat air fryer to 400 F.

Season fillets with salt and black pepper and drizzle some olive oil.

Place in the air fryer basket and AirFry for 10 minutes, flipping once halfway through.

Remove to a plate.

Add pecans and fennel slices to a baking dish.

Drizzle with olive oil and season with salt and black pepper.

Transfer the dish to the fryer and Bake for 5 minutes.

When ready, add balsamic vinegar and olive oil to the mixture, season with salt and black pepper.

Pour over the black cod and serve.

Salmon & Spring Onion Balls

Prep + Cook Time: 15 minutes

2 Servings

INGREDIENTS

1 cup tinned salmon

¼ celery stalk, chopped

1 spring onion, sliced

4 tbsp wheat germ

2 tbsp olive oil

1 large egg

1 tbsp fresh dill, chopped

½ tsp garlic powder

DIRECTIONS

Preheat air fryer to 390 F.

In a large bowl, mix tinned salmon, egg, celery, onion, dill, and garlic.

Shape the mixture into balls and roll them in wheat germ.

Carefully flatten and place in them the greased air fryer basket.

AirFry for 8- 10 minutes, flipping once halfway through until golden.

Serve warm.

Trout with Dill-Yogurt Sauce

Prep + Cook Time: 20 minutes

4 Servings

INGREDIENTS

4 trout pieces

2 tbsp olive oil

Salt to taste

½ cup greek yogurt

2 garlic cloves, minced

2 tbsp fresh dill, finely chopped

DIRECTIONS

Preheat air fryer to 380 F.

Drizzle the trout with olive oil and season with salt.

Place the seasoned trout into the frying basket and AirFry for 12-14 minutes, flipping once.

In a bowl, mix Greek yogurt, garlic, chopped dill, and salt.

Top the trout with the dill sauce and serve.

Rosemary Catfish

Prep + Cook Time: 25 minutes

4 Servings

INGREDIENTS

4 catfish fillets

¼ cup seasoned fish fry

1 tbsp olive oil

1 tbsp fresh rosemary, chopped

DIRECTIONS

Preheat air fryer to 400 F.

Add the seasoned fish fry and the fillets to a large Ziploc bag; massage well to coat.

Place the fillets in the greased frying basket and AirFry for 10-12 minutes.

Flip the fillets and cook for 2-3 more minutes until crispy.

Top with freshly chopped rosemary and serve.

Air-Fried Broiled Tilapia

Prep + Cook Time: 15 minutes

4 Servings

INGREDIENTS

1 lb tilapia fillets

1 tsp old bay seasoning

2 tbsp canola oil

2 tbsp lemon pepper

Salt to taste

2 butter buds

DIRECTIONS

Preheat air fryer to 400 F.

Drizzle canola oil over tilapia. In a bowl, mix salt, lemon pepper, butter buds, and old bay seasoning; spread on the fish.

Place the fillets in the fryer to AirFry for 10-12 minutes, turning once, until crispy.

Serve with green salad.

Japanese Ponzu Marinated Tuna

Prep + Cook Time: 20 minutes + marinating time

4 Servings

INGREDIENTS

4 tuna steaks

1 cup Japanese ponzu sauce

2 tbsp sesame oil

1 tbsp red pepper flakes

2 tbsp ginger paste

¼ cup scallions, sliced

Salt and black pepper to taste

DIRECTIONS

In a bowl, mix the ponzu sauce, sesame oil, red pepper flakes, ginger paste, salt, and black pepper.

Add in the tuna and toss to coat.

Cover and marinate for 60 minutes in the fridge.

Preheat air fryer to 380 F.

Remove tuna from the marinade and arrange on the greased frying basket.

AirFry for 14-16 minutes, turning once.

Top with scallions and serve with green salad.

Delicious Seafood Pie

Prep + Cook Time: 60 minutes + cooling time

4 Servings

INGREDIENTS

1 cup seafood mix

1 lb russet potatoes, peeled and quartered

1 carrot, grated

½ fennel bulb, sliced

2 tbsp fresh parsley, chopped

10 oz baby spinach

1 small tomato, diced

½ celery stick, grated

2 tbsp butter

4 tbsp milk

½ cup cheddar cheese, grated

1 small red chili, minced

Salt and black pepper to taste

DIRECTIONS

Cover the potatoes with salted water in a pot and cook over medium heat for 18 minutes or until tender.

Drain and mash them with butter, milk, salt, and pepper: Mix until smooth and set aside.

In a bowl, mix celery, carrot, red chili, fennel, parsley, seafood mix, tomato, spinach, salt, and black pepper; mix well.

Preheat air fryer to 330 F.

In a casserole baking dish, spread the veggie mixture.

Top with potato mash and level.

Sprinkle with cheddar cheese and place the dish in the air fryer.

Bake for 20-25 minutes until golden and bubbling at the edges.

Let cool for 10 minutes, slice, and serve.

Basil Crab & Potato Patties

Prep + Cook Time: 20 minutes + refrigerating time

4 Servings

INGREDIENTS

3 potatoes, boiled and mashed

1 cup cooked crab meat

¼ cup red onions, chopped

1 tbsp fresh basil, chopped

½ celery stalk, chopped

½ bell red pepper, chopped

1 tbsp Dijon mustard

½ lemon, zested and juiced

¼ cup breadcrumbs

1 tsp old bay seasoning

½ cup mayonnaise

Salt and black pepper to taste

DIRECTIONS

Place mashed potatoes, red onions, old bay seasoning, breadcrumbs, celery, bell pepper, mustard, lemon zest, crab meat, salt, and pepper in a large bowl and mix well.

Make patties from the mixture and refrigerate for 30 minutes.

Mix the mayonnaise, lemon juice, basil, salt, and pepper and set aside.

Preheat air fryer to 390 F.

Remove the patties from the fridge and place them in the greased frying basket.

AirFry for 12-14 minutes, flipping once until golden.

Serve the patties with basil-mayo dip.

Sesame Prawns with Firecracker Sauce

Prep + Cook Time: 20 minutes

4 Servings

INGREDIENTS

1 lb tiger prawns, peeled

Salt and black pepper to taste

2 eggs

½ cup flour

¼ cup sesame seeds

¾ cup seasoned breadcrumbs

Firecracker sauce:

⅓ cup sour cream

2 tbsp buffalo sauce

¼ cup spicy ketchup

1 green onion, chopped

DIRECTIONS

Preheat air fryer to 390 F.

Beat the eggs in a bowl with salt.

In another bowl, mix breadcrumbs with sesame seeds.

In a third bowl, mix flour with salt and pepper.

Dip prawns in the flour and then in the eggs, and finally in the crumbs.

Spray with cooking spray and AirFry for 10 minutes, flipping once.

Meanwhile, mix well all thee sauce ingredients, except for green onion in a bowl.

Serve the prawns with firecracker sauce and scatter with freshly chopped green onions.

Wild Salmon with Creamy Parsley Sauce

Prep + Cook Time: 20 minutes

4 Servings

INGREDIENTS

4 Alaskan wild salmon fillets

2 tsp olive oil

Salt to taste

½ cup heavy cream

½ cup milk

2 tbsp fresh parsley, chopped

DIRECTIONS

Preheat air fryer to 380 F.

Drizzle the fillets with olive oil, and season with salt and black pepper.

Place salmon in the frying basket and Bake for 15 minutes, turning once until tender and crispy.

In a bowl, mix milk, parsley, salt, and whipped cream.

Serve the salmon with the sauce.

Fried Catfish Fillets

Prep + Cook Time: 20 minutes

2 Servings

INGREDIENTS

2 catfish fillets

½ cup breadcrumbs

¼ tsp cayenne pepper

¼ tsp fish seasoning

1 tbsp fresh parsley, chopped

Salt to taste

DIRECTIONS

Preheat air fryer to 400 F.

Pour all the dry ingredients, except for the parsley, in a bowl.

Add in the fish pieces and toss to coat.

Lightly spray the fish with olive oil.

Put the fillets in the fryer basket and AirFry for 6-7 minutes.

Flip and cook further for 5 minutes.

Garnish with freshly chopped parsley and serve.

Peach Salsa & Beer Halibut Tacos

Prep + Cook Time: 15 minutes

4 Servings

INGREDIENTS

4 corn tortillas

1 halibut fillet

2 tbsp olive oil

1 ½ cups flour

1 can beer

A pinch of salt

4 tbsp peach salsa

4 tsp fresh cilantro, chopped

1 tsp baking powder

DIRECTIONS

Preheat air fryer to 390 F.

In a bowl, combine flour, baking powder, and salt.

Pour in some of the beer, enough to form a batter-like consistency.

Save the rest of the beer to gulp with the tacos.

Slice the fillet into 4 strips.

Dip them into the beer batter and arrange on a lined baking dish.

Place in the fryer and AirFry for 8 minutes.

Spread the peach salsa on the tortillas.

Top with fish strips and cilantro to serve.

Crab Fritters with Sweet Chili Sauce

Prep + Cook Time: 20 minutes

4 Servings

INGREDIENTS

1 lb jumbo crabmeat

1 lime, zested and juiced

1 tsp ginger paste

1 tsp garlic puree

1 tbsp fresh cilantro, chopped

1 red chili, roughly chopped

1 egg

¼ cup panko breadcrumbs

1 tsp soy sauce sauce

3 tbsp sweet chili sauce

DIRECTIONS

Preheat air fryer to 400 F.

In a bowl, mix crabmeat, lime zest, egg, ginger paste, and garlic puree.

Form small cakes out of the mixture and dredge them into breadcrumbs.

Place in the greased frying basket and AirFry for 15 minutes, shaking once until golden.

In a small bowl, mix the sweet chili sauce with lime juice and soy sauce.

Serve the fritters topped with cilantro and sweet chili sauce

Ale-Battered Scampi with Tartare Sauce

Prep + Cook Time: 15 minutes

4 Servings

INGREDIENTS

1 lb prawns, peeled and deveined

1 cup plain flour

1 cup ale beer

Salt and black pepper to taste

Tartare sauce:

½ cup mayonnaise

2 tbsp capers, roughly chopped

2 tbsp fresh dill, chopped

1 pickled cucumber, finely chopped

2 tsp lemon juice

½ tsp Worcestershire sauce

DIRECTIONS

Preheat air fryer to 380 F.

In a bowl, mix all the sauce ingredients and keep in the fridge.

Mix flour, ale beer, salt, and pepper in a large bowl.

Dip in the prawns and place them in the frying basket.

AirFry for 10 minutes, shaking halfway through the cooking time.

Serve with the tartare sauce.

Herbed Garlic Lobster

Prep + Cook Time: 15 minutes

4 Servings

INGREDIENTS

4 oz lobster tails, halved

1 garlic clove, minced

1 tbsp butter

Salt and black pepper to taste

½ tbsp lemon Juice

DIRECTIONS

Blend all ingredients, except for lobster, in a food processor.

Clean the skin of the lobster and cover it with the mixture.

Preheat air fryer to 380 F.

Place the lobster in the frying basket and AirFry for 10 minutes, turning once halfway through.

Serve with fresh herbs.

Soy Sauce-Glazed Cod

Prep + Cook Time: 15 minutes

2 Servings

INGREDIENTS

2 cod fillets

1 tbsp olive oil

Salt and black pepper to taste

1 tbsp soy sauce

1 tbsp sesame oil

¼ tsp ginger powder

¼ tsp honey

DIRECTIONS

Preheat air fryer to 370 F.

In a bowl, combine olive oil, salt, and pepper.

Rub the mixture onto the fillets.

Place them on a piece of aluminum sheet and then in the greased frying basket.

Bake for 6 minutes.

Meanwhile, combine the soy sauce, ginger powder, honey, and sesame oil in a small bowl.

Flip the fillets and brush them with the glaze.

Cook for 3 more minutes.

Serve warm.

Pistachio-Crusted Salmon Fillets

Prep + Cook Time: 20 minutes

2 Servings

INGREDIENTS

2 salmon fillets

1 tsp mustard

4 tbsp pistachios, chopped

Salt and black pepper to taste

1 tsp garlic powder

2 tsp lemon juice

2 tbsp Parmesan cheese, grated

1 tsp olive oil

DIRECTIONS

Preheat air fryer to 350 F.

Whisk together mustard, olive oil, lemon juice, salt, black pepper, and garlic powder in a bowl.

Rub the mustard mixture onto salmon fillets.

Combine the pistachios with Parmesan cheese; sprinkle on top of the salmon.

Place the salmon in the greased frying basket, skin side down, and Bake for 12-13 minutes.

Flip at the 7- minute mark.

Serve.

Smoked Trout Frittata

Prep + Cook Time: 25 minutes

4 Servings

INGREDIENTS

2 tbsp olive oil

1 onion, sliced

1 egg, beaten

6 tbsp crème fraiche

½ tbsp horseradish sauce

1 cup smoked trout, diced

2 tbsp fresh dill, chopped

DIRECTIONS

Preheat air fryer to 350 F.

Heat olive oil in a pan over medium heat. Stir-fry onion for 3 minutes.

In a bowl, mix the egg with crème fraiche and horseradish sauce.

Add the onion, dill, and trout and mix well.

Pour the mixture into a greased baking dish and Bake in the fryer for 14 minutes until golden

Effortless Tuna Fritters

Prep + Cook Time: 20 minutes + refrigerating time

2 Servings

INGREDIENTS

5 oz canned tuna

1 tsp lime juice

½ tsp paprika

¼ cup flour

½ cup milk

1 small onion, diced

2 eggs

1 tsp chili powder, optional

½ tsp salt

DIRECTIONS

Place all ingredients in a bowl and mix well.

Make two large patties out of the mixture.

Refrigerate them for 30 minutes.

Then, remove and AirFry the patties for 13-15 minutes at 350 F in the greased frying basket, flipping once halfway through cooking.

Serve warm

Smoked Fish Quiche

Prep + Cook Time: 35 minutes

4 Servings

INGREDIENTS

1 pie crust

5 eggs, lightly beaten

4 tbsp heavy cream

¼ cup green onions, finely chopped

2 tbsp fresh parsley, chopped

1 tsp baking powder

Salt and black pepper to taste

1 lb smoked salmon, chopped

1 cup mozzarella cheese, shrcdded

DIRECTIONS

In a bowl, whisk eggs, heavy cream, green onions, parsley, baking powder, salt, and pepper.

Stir in salmon and mozzarella cheese.

Roll out the pie crust and press it gently into a greased quiche pan that fits in your air fryer.

Prick the pie all over with a fork.

Pour in the salmon mixture and place the pan inside the fryer.

Bake for 25 minutes at 360 F. Let cool slightly before slicing.

Louisiana-Style Shrimp

Prep + Cook Time: 14 minutes

4 Servings

INGREDIENTS

1 lb shrimp, peeled and deveined

1 egg, beaten

1 cup flour

1 cup breadcrumbs

2 tbsp Cajun seasoning

Salt and black pepper to taste

1 lemon, cut into wedges

DIRECTIONS

Preheat air fryer to 390 F.

Spray the air fryer basket with cooking spray.

Beat the eggs in a bowl and season with salt and black pepper.

In a separate bowl, mix breadcrumbs with Cajun seasoning.

In a third bowl, pour the flour.

Dip shrimp in flour, then in the eggs, and finally in the crumbs mixture.

Spray with cooking spray and AirFry in the frying basket for 5 minutes.

Flip and cook for 4 more minutes.

Serve with lemon wedges.

Cajun-Rubbed Jumbo Shrimp

Prep + Cook Time: 15 minutes

2 Servings

INGREDIENTS

1 lb jumbo shrimp, deveined

Salt to taste

¼ tsp old bay seasoning

⅓ tsp smoked paprika

¼ tsp cayenne pepper

1 tbsp olive oil

DIRECTIONS

Preheat air fryer to 390 degrees.

In a bowl, add shrimp, paprika, olive oil, salt, old bay seasoning, and cayenne pepper; mix well.

Place the shrimp in the fryer and AirFry for 8-10 minutes, shaking once.

Herbed Garlic Lobster

Prep + Cook Time: 15 minutes

4 Servings

INGREDIENTS

4 oz lobster tails, halved

1 garlic clove, minced

1 tbsp butter

Salt and black pepper to taste

½ tbsp lemon Juice

DIRECTIONS

Blend all ingredients, except for lobster, in a food processor.

Clean the skin of the lobster and cover it with the mixture.

Preheat air fryer to 380 F.

Place the lobster in the frying basket and AirFry for 10 minutes, turning once halfway through.

Serve with fresh herbs.

Enjoy!

Salmon Cakes

Prep + Cook Time: 15 minutes + marinating time

4 Servings

INGREDIENTS

1 lb cooked salmon

4 potatoes, boiled and mashed

½ cup flour

2 tbsp capers, chopped

2 tbsp fresh parsley, chopped

1 tbsp olive oil

Zest of 1 lemon

DIRECTIONS

Place mashed potatoes in a bowl and flake the salmon over.

Stir in capers, parsley, and lemon zest.

Shape cakes out of the mixture and dust them with flour.

Refrigerate for 1 hour.

Preheat the air fryer to 350 F.

Remove the cakes and brush them with olive oil.

Bake in the greased frying basket for 12-14 minutes, flipping once halfway through cooking.

Serve with ketchup.

Enjoy!

Parmesan Tilapia Fillets

Prep + Cook Time: 15 minutes

4 Servings

INGREDIENTS

¾ cup Parmesan cheese, grated

2 tbsp olive oil

2 tsp paprika

2 tbsp fresh parsley, chopped

¼ tsp garlic powder

4 tilapia fillets

DIRECTIONS

Preheat air fryer to 350 F.

Mix parsley, Parmesan cheese, garlic, and paprika in a shallow bowl.

Coat fillets with the Parmesan mixture and brush with the olive oil.

Place the filets into the air fryer basket and AirFry for 10-12 minutes, flipping once until golden brown.

Serve immediately

Spicy Shrimp with Coconut-Avocado Dip

Prep + Cook Time: 15 minutes

4 Servings

INGREDIENTS

1 ¼ lb tiger shrimp, peeled and deveined

2 garlic cloves, minced

¼ tsp red chili flakes

1 lime, juiced and zested

Salt to taste

1 tbsp fresh cilantro, chopped

1 large avocado, pitted

¼ cup coconut cream

2 tablespoons olive oil

DIRECTIONS

Blend avocado, lime juice, coconut cream, cilantro, olive oil, and salt in a food processor until smooth.

Transfer to a bowl, cover, and keep in the fridge until ready to use.

Preheat air fryer to 390 F.

In a bowl, place garlic, chili flakes, lime zest, and salt, and add in the shrimp; toss to coat.

Place them in the frying basket and AirFry for 8-10 minutes, shaking once halfway through or until entirely pink.

Serve with the chilled avocado dip.

Calamari Rings with Olives

Prep + Cook Time: 30 minutes

4 Servings

INGREDIENTS

1 lb calamari rings

2 tbsp cilantro, chopped

1 chili pepper, minced

2 tbsp olive oil

1 cup pimiento-stuffed green olives

Salt and black pepper to taste

DIRECTIONS

In a bowl, add calamari rings, chili pepper, salt, black pepper, olive oil, and fresh cilantro.

Marinate for 10 minutes.

Pour the calamari into a baking dish and place it inside the fryer.

AirFry for 15 minutes, stirring every 5 minutes at 400 F.

Serve warm with pimiento-stuffed olives.

Cajun Mango Salmon

Prep + Cook Time: 15 minutes

4 Servings

INGREDIENTS

4 salmon fillets

½ tsp brown sugar

1 tbsp Cajun seasoning

1 lemon, zested and juiced

1 tbsp fresh parsley, chopped

2 tbsp mango salsa

DIRECTIONS

Preheat air fryer to 350 F.

In a bowl, mix sugar, Cajun seasoning, lemon juice and zest, and coat the salmon with the mixture.

Line with parchment paper the frying basket and place in the fish.

Bake for 12 minutes, turning once halfway through.

Top with parsley and mango salsa to serve.

Fried Tilapia Bites

Prep + Cook Time: 20 minutes

4 Servings

INGREDIENTS

1 lb tilapia fillets, cut into chunks

½ cup cornflakes

1 cup flour

2 eggs, beaten

Salt to taste

Lemon wedges for serving

DIRECTIONS

Preheat air fryer to 390 F.

Pour the flour, eggs, and cornflakes each into different bowls.

Dip the tilapia first in the flour, then in the egg, and lastly, coat with the cornflakes.

Lay on the greased air fryer basket and AirFry for 6 minutes.

 Shake and cook for 4-5 minutes until crispy.

Serve with lemon wedges.

Enjoy!

Salmon Bowl with Lime Drizzle

Prep + Cook Time: 15 minutes

3 Servings

INGREDIENTS

1 pound salmon steak

2 teaspoons sesame oil

Sea salt and Sichuan pepper, to taste

1/2 teaspoon coriander seeds

1 lime, juiced

2 tablespoons reduced-sodium soy sauce

1 teaspoon honey

DIRECTIONS

Pat the salmon dry and drizzle it with 1 teaspoon of sesame oil.

Season the salmon with salt, pepper and coriander seeds.

Transfer the salmon to the Air Fryer cooking basket.

Cook the salmon at 400 degrees F for 5 minutes; turn the salmon over and continue to cook for 5 minutes more or until opaque.

Meanwhile, warm the remaining ingredients in a small saucepan to make the lime drizzle.

Slice the fish into bite-sized strips, drizzle with the sauce and serve immediately.

Enjoy!

Classic Calamari with Mediterranean Sauce

Prep + Cook Time: 10 minutes

2 Servings

INGREDIENTS

1/2 pound calamari tubes cut into rings, cleaned

Sea salt and ground black pepper, to season

1/2 cup almond flour

1/2 cup all-purpose flour

4 tablespoons parmesan cheese, grated

1/2 cup ale beer

1/4 teaspoon cayenne pepper

1/2 cup breadcrumbs

1/4 cup mayonnaise

1/4 cup Greek-style yogurt

1 clove garlic, minced

1 tablespoon fresh lemon juice

1 teaspoon fresh parsley, chopped

1 teaspoon fresh dill, chopped

DIRECTIONS

Sprinkle the calamari with salt and black pepper.

Mix the flour, cheese and beer in a bowl until well combined.

In another bowl, mix cayenne pepper and breadcrumbs.

Dip the calamari pieces in the flour mixture, then roll them onto the breadcrumb mixture, pressing to coat on all sides; transfer them to a lightly oiled cooking basket.

Cook at 400 degrees F for 4 minutes, shaking the basket halfway through the cooking time.

Meanwhile, mix the remaining ingredients until everything is well incorporated.

Serve warm calamari with the sauce for dipping.

Enjoy!

Herb and Garlic Grouper Filets

Prep + Cook Time: 15 minutes

3 Servings

INGREDIENTS

1 pound grouper filets

1/4 teaspoon shallot powder

1/4 teaspoon porcini powder

1 teaspoon fresh garlic, minced

1/2 teaspoon cayenne pepper

1/2 teaspoon hot paprika

1/4 teaspoon oregano

1/2 teaspoon marjoram

1/2 teaspoon sage

1 tablespoon butter, melted

Sea salt and black pepper, to taste

DIRECTIONS

Pat dry the grouper filets using kitchen towels.

In a small dish, make the rub by mixing the remaining ingredients until everything is well incorporated.

Rub the fish with the mixture, coating well on all sides.

Cook the grouper filets in the preheated Air Fryer at 400 degrees F for 5 minutes; turn the filets over and cook on the other side for 5 minutes more.

Serve over hot rice if desired.

Enjoy!

Crab Cake Burgers

Prep + Cook Time: 2hours 20 minutes

3 Servings

INGREDIENTS

2 eggs, beaten

1 shallot, chopped

2 garlic cloves, crushed

1 tablespoon olive oil

1 teaspoon yellow mustard

1 teaspoon fresh cilantro, chopped

10 ounces crab meat

1 cup tortilla chips, crushed

1/2 teaspoon cayenne pepper

1/2 teaspoon ground black pepper

Sea salt, to taste

3/4 cup fresh bread crumbs

DIRECTIONS

In a mixing bowl, thoroughly combine the eggs, shallot, garlic, olive oil, mustard, cilantro, crab meat, tortilla chips, cayenne pepper, black pepper, and salt. Mix until well combined.

Shape the mixture into 6 patties.

Dip the crab patties into the fresh breadcrumbs, coating well on all sides.

Place in your refrigerator for 2 hours.

Spritz the crab patties with cooking oil on both sides.

Cook in the preheated Air Fryer at 360 degrees F for 14 minutes.

Serve on dinner rolls if desired. Enjoy!

Cajun Cod Fillets with Avocado Sauce

Prep + Cook Time: 20 minutes

2 Servings

INGREDIENTS

2 cod fish fillets

1 egg Sea salt, to taste

1/2 cup tortilla chips, crushed

2 teaspoons olive oil

1/2 avocado, peeled, pitted, and mashed

1 tablespoon mayonnaise

3 tablespoons sour cream

1/2 teaspoon yellow mustard

1 teaspoon lemon juice

1 garlic clove, minced

1/4 teaspoon black pepper

1/4 teaspoon salt

1/4 teaspoon hot pepper sauce

DIRECTIONS

Start by preheating your Air Fryer to 360 degrees F.

Spritz the Air Fryer basket with cooking oil.

Pat dry the fish fillets with a kitchen towel.

Beat the egg in a shallow bowl.

In a separate bowl, thoroughly combine the salt, crushed tortilla chips, and olive oil.

Dip the fish into the egg, then, into the crumb mixture, making sure to coat thoroughly.

Cook in the preheated Air Fryer approximately 12 minutes.

Meanwhile, make the avocado sauce by mixing the remaining ingredients in a bowl.

Place in your refrigerator until ready to serve.

Serve the fish fillets with chilled avocado sauce on the side.

Enjoy!

Snapper Casserole with Gruyere Cheese

Prep + Cook Time: 25 minutes

4 Servings

INGREDIENTS

2 tablespoons olive oil

1 shallot, thinly sliced

2 garlic cloves, minced 1

½ pounds snapper fillets

Sea salt and ground black pepper, to taste

1 teaspoon cayenne pepper

1/2 teaspoon dried basil

1/2 cup tomato puree

1/2 cup white wine

1 cup Gruyere cheese, shredded

DIRECTIONS

Heat 1 tablespoon of olive oil in a saucepan over medium-high heat.

Now, cook the shallot and garlic until tender and aromatic.

Preheat your Air Fryer to 370 degrees F.

Grease a casserole dish with 1 tablespoon of olive oil.

Place the snapper fillet in the casserole dish.

Season with salt, black pepper, and cayenne pepper.

Add the sautéed shallot mixture.

Add the basil, tomato puree and wine to the casserole dish.

Cook for 10 minutes in the preheated Air Fryer.

Top with the shredded cheese and cook an additional 7 minutes.

Serve immediately

Halibut with Thai Lemongrass Marinade

Prep + Cook Time: 45 minutes

2 Servings

INGREDIENTS

2 tablespoons tamari sauce

2 tablespoons fresh lime juice

2 tablespoons olive oil

1 teaspoon Thai curry paste

1/2 inch lemongrass, finely chopped

1 teaspoon basil

2 cloves garlic, minced

2 tablespoons shallot, minced

Sea salt and ground black pepper, to taste

2 halibut steaks

DIRECTIONS

Place all ingredients in a ceramic dish; let it marinate for 30 minutes.

Place the halibut steaks in the lightly greased cooking basket.

Bake in the preheated Air Fryer at 400 degrees F for 9 to 10 minutes, basting with the reserved marinade and flipping them halfway through the cooking time.

Enjoy!

Tuna Cake Burgers with Beer Cheese Sauce

Prep + Cook Time: 2hours 20 minutes

4 Servings

INGREDIENTS

1 pound canned tuna, drained

1 egg, whisked

1 garlic clove, minced

2 tablespoons shallots, minced

1 cup fresh breadcrumbs

Sea salt and ground black pepper, to taste

1 tablespoon sesame oil

Beer Cheese Sauce:

1 tablespoon butter

1 cup beer

1 tablespoon rice flour

2 tablespoons Colby cheese, grated

DIRECTIONS

In a mixing bowl, thoroughly combine the tuna, egg, garlic, shallots, breadcrumbs, salt, and black pepper.

Shape the tuna mixture into four patties and place in your refrigerator for 2 hours.

Brush the patties with sesame oil on both sides.

Cook in the preheated Air Fryer at 360 degrees F for 14 minutes.

In the meantime, melt the butter in a pan over a moderate heat.

Add the beer and flour and whisk until it starts bubbling.

Now, stir in the grated cheese and cook for 3 to 4 minutes longer or until the cheese has melted.

Spoon the sauce over the fish cake burgers and serve immediately.

Easiest Lobster Tails Ever

Prep + Cook Time: 10 minutes

2 Servings

INGREDIENTS

2 6-ounce lobster tails

1 teaspoon fresh cilantro, minced

1/2 teaspoon dried rosemary

1/2 teaspoon garlic, pressed

1 teaspoon deli mustard

Sea salt and ground black pepper, to taste

1 teaspoon olive oil

DIRECTIONS

Toss the lobster tails with the other ingredients until they are well coated on all sides.

Cook the lobster tails at 370 degrees F for 3 minutes.

Then, turn them and cook on the other side for 3 to 4 minutes more until they are opaque. Serve warm and enjoy!

Grouper with Miso-Honey Sauce

Prep + Cook Time: 15 minutes

2 Servings

INGREDIENTS

3/4 pound grouper fillets

Salt and white pepper, to taste

1 tablespoon sesame oil

1 teaspoon water

 1 teaspoon deli mustard or Dijon mustard

1/4 cup white miso

1 tablespoon mirin

1 tablespoon honey

1 tablespoon Shoyu sauce

DIRECTIONS

Sprinkle the grouper fillets with salt and white pepper; drizzle them with a nonstick cooking oil.

Cook the fish at 400 degrees F for 5 minutes; turn the fish fillets over and cook an additional 5 minutes.

Meanwhile, make the sauce by whisking the remaining ingredients.

Serve the warm fish with the miso-honey sauce on the side.

Southwestern Prawns with Asparagus

Prep + Cook Time: 10 minutes

3 Servings

INGREDIENTS

1 pound prawns, deveined

1/2 pound asparagus spears, cut into1-inch chinks

1 teaspoon butter, melted

1/4 teaspoon oregano

1/2 teaspoon mixed peppercorns, crushed

Salt, to taste

1 ripe avocado

1 lemon, sliced

1/2 cup chunky-style salsa

DIRECTIONS

Toss your prawns and asparagus with melted butter, oregano, salt and mixed peppercorns.

Cook the prawns and asparagus at 400 degrees F for 5 minutes, shaking the basket halfway through the cooking time.

Divide the prawns and asparagus between serving plates and garnish with avocado and lemon slices.

Serve with the salsa on the side.

Enjoy!

Homemade Fish Fingers

Prep + Cook Time: 15 minutes

2 Servings

INGREDIENTS

3/4 pound tilapia

1 egg

2 tablespoons milk

4 tablespoons chickpea flour

1/4 cup pork rinds

1/2 cup breadcrumbs

1/2 teaspoon red chili flakes

Coarse sea salt and black pepper, to season

DIRECTIONS

Rinse the tilapia and pat it dry using kitchen towels.

Then, cut the tilapia into strips.

Then, whisk the egg, milk and chickpea flour in a rimmed plate.

Add the pork rinds and breadcrumbs to another plate; stir in red chili flakes, salt and black pepper and stir to combine well.

Dip the fish strips in the egg mixture, then, roll them over the breadcrumb mixture.

Transfer the fish fingers to the Air Fryer cooking basket and spritz them with a nonstick cooking spray.

Cook in the preheated Air Fryer at 400 degrees F for 10 minutes, shaking the basket halfway through to ensure even browning.

Serve warm and enjoy.

Dijon Catfish with Eggplant Sauce

Prep + Cook Time: 30 minutes

3 Servings

INGREDIENTS

1 pound catfish fillets

Sea salt and ground black pepper, to taste

1/4 cup Dijon mustard

1 tablespoon honey

1 tablespoon white vinegar

1 pound eggplant,

1 ½-inch cubes

2 tablespoons olive oil

1 tablespoon tahini

1/2 teaspoon garlic, minced

1 tablespoon parsley, chopped

DIRECTIONS

Pat the catfish dry with paper towels and generously season with salt and black pepper.

In a small mixing bowl, thoroughly combine Dijon mustard, honey and vinegar.

Cook the fish in your Air Fryer at 400 degrees F for 5 minutes.

Turn the fish over and brush with the Dijon mixture; continue to cook for a further 5 minutes.

Then, set your Air Fryer to 400 degrees F.

Add the eggplant chunks to the cooking basket and cook for 15 minutes, shaking the basket occasionally to ensure even cooking.

Transfer the cooked eggplant to a bowl of your food processor; stir in the remaining ingredients and blitz until everything is well blended and smooth.

Serve the warm catfish with the eggplant sauce on the side.

Scallops with Pineapple Salsa and Pickled Onions

Prep + Cook Time: 15 minutes

3 Servings

INGREDIENTS

12 scallops

1 teaspoon sesame oil

1/4 teaspoon dried rosemary

1/2 teaspoon dried tarragon

1/2 teaspoon dried basil

1/4 teaspoon red pepper flakes, crushed

Coarse sea salt and black pepper, to taste

1/2 cup pickled onions, drained

Pineapple Salsa:

1 cup pineapple, diced

2 tablespoons fresh cilantro, roughly chopped

1 jalapeño, deveined and minced

1 small-sized red onion, minced

1 teaspoon ginger root, peeled and grated

1/2 teaspoon coconut sugar

Sea salt and ground black pepper, to taste

DIRECTIONS

Toss the scallops sesame oil, rosemary, tarragon, basil, red pepper, salt and black pepper.

Cook in the preheated Air Fryer at 400 degrees F for 6 to 7 minutes, shaking the basket once or twice to ensure even cooking.

Meanwhile, process all the salsa ingredients in your blender; cover and place the salsa in your refrigerator until ready to serve.

Serve the warm scallops with pickled onions and pineapple salsa on the side.

Enjoy!

Korean-Style Salmon Patties

Prep + Cook Time: 15 minutes

4 Servings

INGREDIENTS

1 pound salmon

1 egg

1 garlic clove, minced

2 green onions, minced

1/2 cup rolled oats

 Sauce:

1 teaspoon rice wine

1 ½ tablespoons soy sauce

1 teaspoon honey

A pinch of salt

1 teaspoon gochugaru

Korean red chili pepper flakes

DIRECTIONS

Start by preheating your Air Fryer to 380 degrees F.

Spritz the Air Fryer basket with cooking oil.

Mix the salmon, egg, garlic, green onions, and rolled oats in a bowl; knead with your hands until everything is well incorporated.

Shape the mixture into equally sized patties.

Transfer your patties to the Air Fryer basket.

Cook the fish patties for 10 minutes, turning them over halfway through.

Meanwhile, make the sauce by whisking all ingredients.

Serve the warm fish patties with the sauce on the side.

Enjoy!

.

Ingram Content Group UK Ltd.
Milton Keynes UK
UKHW021814100323
418362UK00001B/32